WILE E. COYOTE
EXPERIMENTS WITH
SPEED AND VELOCITY

ACME CO.

ZOOM!

by MARK WEAKLAND
illustrated by PACO SORDO

CAPSTONE PRESS
a capstone imprint

Published in 2017 by Capstone Press
A Capstone Imprint
1710 Roe Crest Drive
North Mankato, Minnesota 56003
www.mycapstone.com

Library of Congress Cataloging-in-Publication Data
Names: Weakland, Mark, author. | Sordo, Paco, illustrator.
Title: Zoom! : Wile E. Coyote experiments with speed and velocity /
by Mark Weakland ; illustrated by Paco Sordo.
Description: North Mankato, Minnesota : Capstone Press, [2017] | Series:
Warner Brothers. Wile E. Coyote, physical science genius | Includes bibliographical references and index.
Identifiers: LCCN 2016037087| ISBN 9781515737346 (library binding) | ISBN 9781515737384 (pbk.) |
ISBN 9781515737506 (ebook (pdf)
Subjects: LCSH: Speed—Experiments--Juvenile literature. | Dynamics—Experiments—Juvenile literature.
| Science—Experiments—Juvenile literature. | Wile E. Coyote (Fictitious character)—Juvenile literature.
Classification: LCC QC137.52 .W4325 2017 | DDC 531.112—dc23
LC record available at https://lccn.loc.gov/2016037087

Editorial Credits
Michelle Hasselius, editor; Ashlee Suker, designer; Steve Walker, production specialist

Capstone Press thanks Paul Ohmann, PhD, Associate Professor of Physics at the University of St. Thomas
for his help creating this book.

TABLE OF CONTENTS

The Need for Speed

Look at Wile E. run! If he moved a bit faster, he could catch Road Runner. Oh! Road Runner changed direction. That bird can turn on a dime.

Road Runner
(Speedius birdius)

Racing and chasing are all about speed and velocity. Wile E. needs speed to beat Road Runner in a race. To follow Road Runner as he swerves, Wile E. needs to match Road Runner's velocity. If Wile E. knew more about speed and velocity, he could catch his quick-footed enemy.

Coyote
(Hungrius carnivorii)

Let's watch Wile E. go through his motions.
Maybe he'll learn a thing or two.

Talk about running in circles! Wile E. is moving fast, but he's not really going anywhere.

Speed and velocity are part of the study of **motion.** Motion means a change in position. All motion is relative to a fixed point. Right now Wile E. and Road Runner are moving very fast, changing their positions very quickly. They move along a fixed path, past stationary signs.

Some might say both of them have great speed and velocity. People use the words "speed" and "velocity" as if they mean the same thing. They are related, but there is a difference between the two. Speed is how fast something is going. Velocity is speed plus a direction of motion.

motion—the action or process of moving or changing position

CHAPTER 1

FULL SPEED AHEAD

Speed

To catch Road Runner, Wile E. needs to know how fast the bird is going. He uses a radar gun to measure Road Runner's speed.

Speed is a measurement of how fast an object moves. The measurement is made up of two things—**distance** and time.

Distance is how far something travels. If a bird like Road Runner has a speed of 80 miles (129 kilometers) per hour, it can move a distance of 80 miles (129 km) in one hour.

speed = 0 mph

One more thing must be considered to measure speed—the reference point. For speed the reference point is usually the ground. If Wile E. walks at a speed of 3 mph (4.8 km/h), he is being compared to a road sign or another point that is at rest on the ground. Before Road Runner started running, he was standing still. His speed was zero. But after a few seconds, his speed was 80 mph (129 km/h).

speed = 80 mph

One of the first scientists to measure speed as distance over time was Galileo. More than 350 years ago, Galileo let balls roll down a ramp. As they rolled, he observed their motion. Galileo measured how far each ball moved within a certain amount of time. Today people use tools such as radar guns and anemometers to measure speed.

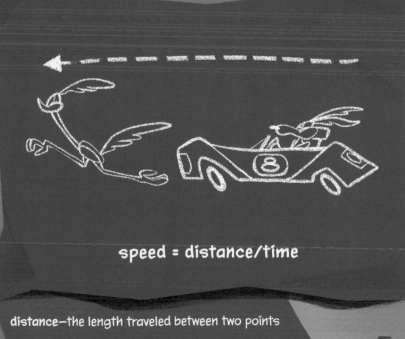

speed = distance/time

distance—the length traveled between two points

Measuring Speed

Wile E. has some serious speed. But he still can't catch the bird. How many miles per hour does Wile E. need to go?

In the United States, speed on the highway is measured in miles per hour, or mph. But scientists measure speed in meters per second, or m/s. The speed of many things, including sound waves, spacecraft, and even light are measured in m/s. Speed through the air and across water is different though. Air and water speed are typically measured in knots. One knot is equal to traveling 1 nautical mile (1.15 miles) in one hour.

100 mph

Average and Instantaneous Speed

Wile E. has a plan to travel faster. But he is making a mistake.
He doesn't understand there are two kinds of speed.

Average speed describes the distance an object travels in a given amount
of time. Let's say Road Runner ran for one hour. In that time he covered
400 miles (644 km). This means his average speed was 400 mph
(644 km/h). During that hour he may have increased or decreased
his speed. Maybe he slowed down to 395 mph (636 km/h) for a few
seconds. Maybe he sped up to 410 mph (660 km/h) for a few seconds.
At the end of the hour, he traveled a total of 400 miles (644 km). So his
average speed was 400 mph (644 km/h).

80 mph

The fastest possible speed in the universe is the speed of light in a vacuum, like outer space. Light speed is 299,792,458 meters per second. That's fast! The speed of light can also be written 186,282 miles per second. That's right, not miles per hour, but miles per second! If you could travel at the speed of light, you could fly to the moon in less than one and a half seconds! Nothing can travel faster than light, not even Road Runner.

When light enters objects such as water or glass, it bends and slows down. This process is called refraction.

Instantaneous speed is different. It is the speed of an object at a given moment. Right now Road Runner is traveling at 415 mph (668 km/h). But in the next moment, he may slow down to 405 mph (652 km/h). After that he may speed up to 417 mph (671 km/h). At each moment, he has a different instantaneous speed.

Wile E. goofed when he confused average speed with instantaneous speed. He also goofed when he thought sitting on a rocket was a good idea!

average speed—the distance an object has traveled divided by the time it has taken to travel that distance

instantaneous speed—the speed of an object at a given moment in time

Common Uses for Speed Measurement

It's useful to know an object's speed. Wile E. understands this. If he knows how fast a rock is traveling, he may be able to duck in time. Or he may not!

Knowing an object's speed comes in handy in everyday life. Pilots use their knowledge of speed to help them safely fly their planes. People measure wind speed to help predict weather. Truck drivers use their average speed to figure out when they will arrive at their final destinations. Police officers calculate a car's instantaneous speed to find out if the driver is breaking the speed limit.

CHAPTER 2

VIVA VELOCITY!

What Is Velocity?

Wile E. now knows about speed. But does he know anything about velocity? Let's find out.

Velocity is speed with direction. To find Road Runner's velocity, Wile E. must know Road Runner's speed and direction. Like speed, velocity is measured in meters per second. But velocity's measurement also gives an object's direction. For example, Wile E. is traveling at a velocity of 75 m/s, west. Road Runner is traveling at a velocity of 75 m/s, east. They have the same speed but different velocities.

Wile E. has the right speed for catching Road Runner. But he isn't traveling in the right direction. In the end Wile E. has only one direction to go. Down!

Average and Instantaneous Velocity

While trying to make a tar pit trap, Wile E. got his drill bit stuck. Now the drill's motor is spinning him at a speed of 13 m/s. This means that he travels a distance of 13 meters every second.

Wile E.'s head is really spinning. He knows velocity has to do with a change in position. And boy, is he changing position! But because he is moving in a circle, Wile E. keeps coming back to the same spot. So his average velocity is zero. However Wile E.'s instantaneous velocity is definitely not zero, since he is moving.

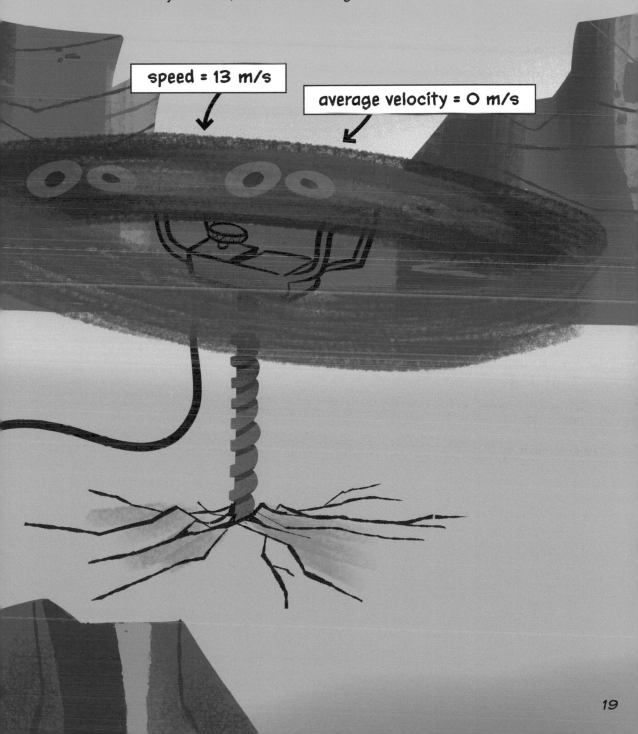

speed = 13 m/s

average velocity = 0 m/s

Acceleration

Wile E. hasn't had much luck catching Road Runner. The bird can go from 0 to 60 mph (97 km/h) in three seconds flat! To catch his speedy enemy, Wile E. needs to accelerate quickly. He thinks his new ACME Super Rocket will help him do just that.

During **acceleration**, a moving object's velocity changes. Acceleration often describes how much speed an object is picking up. Newton's Second Law of Motion says a force, like a push, causes an object to accelerate. The larger the force, the more the object's acceleration will increase.

Acceleration can be measured every second. Take Wile E. on his rocket, for example. In the first second, his rocket is moving at a speed of 5 m/s. In the next second, its speed is 10 m/s. And in the third second, the rocket is moving at 15 m/s. The rocket's speed increased every second. This means it was accelerating. Because Wile E. was sitting on the rocket, he was accelerating too.

Will Wile E. keep accelerating? And if he does, where will he end up?

acceleration—the rate of change of the velocity of a moving object

Deceleration

As Wile E.'s rocket runs out of fuel, it **decelerates**. In other words, it slows down. Poor Wile E.!

Here comes Wile E. on his rocket. At first he is moving at 25 m/s. A second later he is moving at 20 m/s. And a second after that, his speed is 15 m/s.

deceleration—a decrease in the velocity of a moving object

At every second of Wile E.'s motion, his speed was different. This looks a lot like acceleration. The difference is his speed is decreasing, not increasing. Wile E. is slowing down due to the force of **friction**. Until he falls off a cliff, that is!

friction—a force produced when two objects rub against each other; friction slows down objects

Wile E. is confused. Should he be thinking about distance or position?

A change in position is known as **displacement**. Displacement tells how far something moves in a specific direction. To get from point A to point B, Road Runner runs along a winding road. He travels 20 miles (32 km).

displacement—the shortest distance between two points

But a straight line shows his true change in position. The line starts at point A and ends at point B. If Road Runner runs this straight line, he only travels 9 miles (14 km). Nine miles (14 km) is his displacement, or his overall change in position. The average velocity is the displacement divided by the time it takes to get from point A to point B.

Common Uses for Velocity Measurement

An object's velocity is a very useful thing to know. Soldiers calculate velocity to make sure shells fired from big guns hit their targets. Wile E. could learn a thing or two from them!

Pilots use velocity to land airplanes. Rocket scientists calculate velocity all the time. They need to know a space probe's velocity before it can orbit Jupiter or Mars.

Passing a football has to do with velocity too. A quarterback judges how fast to throw the ball and in what direction to throw it. Think about when you play dodgeball at school. Every time someone throws a ball at you, you unconsciously calculate the speed and direction that the ball is moving so you don't get hit!

Speed and Velocity Matter

Can a speedboat help Wile E. catch Road Runner? Not if he's traveling in the wrong direction.

Even though Wile E. was often heading the wrong way, he still learned a lot. He learned that speed and velocity are two different things. Speed is about distance and time. Velocity is about distance, time, and direction.

It can be useful to know your speed and velocity. Drivers check their highway speed. If they are going too fast, they'll get a ticket. Pilots check their air velocity. If they come in from the wrong direction, they can't land safely.

Wile E. should be checking his speed and velocity too. It's the only way he'll ever catch Road Runner!

GLOSSARY

acceleration (ak-sel-uh-RAY-shuhn)—the rate of change of the velocity of a moving object

average speed (AV-uh-rij SPEED)—the distance an object has traveled divided by the time it has taken to travel that distance

deceleration (dee-sell-uh-RAY-shuhn)—a decrease in the velocity of a moving object

displacement (dis-PLAYS-muhnt)—the shortest distance between two points

distance (DIS-tuhns)—the length traveled between two points

instantaneous speed (IN-stuhnt-AY-nee-uhs SPEED)—the speed of an object at a given moment in time

motion (MOH-shuhn)—the action or process of moving or changing position

READ MORE

Clement, Nathan. *Speed.* Honesdale, Penn: Boyds Mills Press, 2013.

Hirsch, Rebecca. *Motion and Forces.* Science Lab. Ann Arbor, Mich.: Cherry Lake Pub., 2012.

Sohn, Emily. *Experiments in Forces and Motion with Toys and Everyday Stuff.* Fun Science. North Mankato, Minn.: Capstone Press, 2016.

INTERNET SITES

FactHound offers a safe, fun way to find Internet sites related to this book. All of the sites on FactHound have been researched by our staff.

Here's all you do:

Visit *www.facthound.com*

Type in this code: 9781515737346

Super-cool stuff!

Check out projects, games and lots more at
www.capstonekids.com

INDEX

OTHER BOOKS IN THIS SERIES

WILE E. COYOTE EXPERIMENTS WITH CHEMICAL REACTIONS

Wile E. Coyote Experiments with ENERGY

WHOOSH! WILE E. COYOTE EXPERIMENTS WITH FLIGHT AND GRAVITY

CLANG! WILE E. COYOTE EXPERIMENTS WITH MAGNETISM